CHI
ONLINE

websites

REACH OUT

LAURA TRENEER

BRF

The Bible Reading Fellowship
15 The Chambers, Vineyard
Abingdon OX14 3FE
brf.org.uk

The Bible Reading Fellowship (BRF) is a Registered Charity (233280)

ISBN 978 0 85746 552 8
First published 2017
10 9 8 7 6 5 4 3 2 1 0
All rights reserved

Acknowledgements

Scripture quotations taken from The Holy Bible, New International
Version (Anglicised edition) copyright © 1979, 1984, 2011 by
Biblica. Used by permission of Hodder & Stoughton Publishers,
a Hachette UK company. All rights reserved. 'NIV' is a registered
trademark of Biblica. UK trademark number 1448790.

A catalogue record for this book is available from the British Library

Printed and bound by CPI Group (UK) Ltd, Croydon CR0 4YY

Contents

'Balanced, supportive, encouraging, practical… A total thumbs up!'

Dr Bex Lewis, author of *Raising Children in a Digital Age*

'An essential resource for all church leaders.'

Jo Swinney, editor of *Preach* magazine

Introduction

Does your church have a website?

- Yes—but it's woefully out of date.
- Yes—but I know it could be better.
- No—and someone gave me this book in the hope that it would convince me that it's really simple and worthwhile, but I'm not so sure…

This series of books starts from the understanding that it is primarily and ultimately God who communicates. He has equipped us to take part. Digital tools are a gift for this, and so are all the traditional church communication methods, but they're more effective when used together. A church can run all sorts of events and groups, but it's a waste of time if no one hears about them. This is where digital communication comes into its own.

Imagine this is you: you walk past the same church on the way back from work every day. Yes, it does meld with the landscape. But you've always secretly wondered what goes on behind those slightly grand doors, and what it looks like inside. You always read that crumbling noticeboard in the vague hope that something might catch your eye and show signs of life. You like the idea of God. You don't know enough about Jesus to be sure. Now and again you idly search online for what your local church is doing. You've never had a friend who goes to church. Like millions of others, you'd happily go if you were invited—but you've never been invited. Perhaps this Christmas…

Churches have an immense opportunity! Not only do they get to be places of sacramental worship, teaching, communion, fellowship and all those other words that are understood by most UK Christians, but not necessarily by their neighbours. They also get to be lights in their community and centres of communication about what it is to be a follower of Christ.

Churches get to ask the big questions in the public sphere. Through every means of communication we have available to us—buildings, services, ministries, websites, printed invitations, social media, videos, magazines, news sheets, noticeboards, the smiles on our faces, the words out of our mouths—churches can fundamentally change perceptions of Jesus Christ and of those who believe he still has the power to change lives.

This series is for those who feel responsibility for church communications and for those who think it makes a difference. There is plenty that the world of corporate and charity marketing can teach the church. Free resources are more readily available than ever before. The options can seem overwhelming—but time, budget and, let's face it, imagination can be limited.

Hopefully the tools in these books will help you form a simple strategy and plan that starts squarely in the reality of your situation. It's written so that the intimidated can relax, the curious can explore and the goal-oriented can focus.

1

Why it matters

I went to a Christian Resources Exhibition one year in London, and got an Uber cab afterwards to the hotel. The driver asked where I'd been. I tried to explain the concept of an exhibition hall full of organisations trying to help churches: 'You know, people who provide training, or chairs, or websites…' He was incredulous. 'Websites? *Churches* with websites?' 'Yes! And they're on social media too.' 'What? *Vicars?* On *Twitter*?' This struck him as incomprehensible and hilarious. I really hope he went home, googled 'church website' or 'church Facebook' out of pure storytelling mirth, and discovered something that blew away his assumptions.

There are plenty within the church who'd identify with my taxi driver. They would say this stuff is irrelevant; perhaps, if pressed, they might even assert that it's not part of the church's calling. They might be described as 'the unwilling'. However, you have chosen to pick up a book with both 'websites' and 'church' in the title. You have already squared what the driver saw as a crazy juxtaposition.

So perhaps you are in a second group: 'the willing'. What would the church do without the willing? You've come to terms with the concept that church requires an online presence. You might say that websites and social media are a tedious, time-consuming necessity, but you accept that the issue needs 'tackling' and 'sorting'.

A warning for the willing—this isn't something that can be fully tackled or sorted in one hit (just as preaching, or a magazine, or any kind of active communication can't be done in a moment). Chapter 3 contains more on how to move from quick progress to sustainability.

Or, finally, perhaps you're excited by the potential in the whole area of digital communication and you feel that such a short book could never cover the breadth and depth of the subject. Plus, this is a printed book! Old school! However, you'll find much here that affirms what you already know, and hopefully some things that will enable you to encourage others to explore. You are 'the curious'.

The risk for the curious is in being overwhelmed by the potential, to the point where you can no longer see the worth of what you already have. You might know how cool your website could be, but being too harsh about the current reality may just hurt someone's feelings unnecessarily. As we see time and again in the example of Christ himself, leading others with vision begins with really knowing, really loving and ultimately serving the people you are with.

So, we have three broad groups: the unwilling, the willing and the curious.

The church can be inward-looking. We can easily see the weaknesses of those who are in our 'body of Christ': the weak legs, the overly forceful thumb, the emotional brain or the pernickety eye. When we look outside and focus on the people we're trying to reach, we find the same groups: those *unwilling* to acknowledge the presence of the church, let alone listen to it, the *willing* and the *curious*. If all our communications are focused on the curious, we may be missing an enormous opportunity.

Recent research asked UK adults how they perceive Christians and the church.[1] It demonstrated that a connection with church still has an important part to play in many people's spiritual journeys. Other research, by the University of Lancaster, identified 13% as anti-religious.[2] The New Atheists punch above their weight in the public consciousness.

The church can hear their voice as the voice of the mockers. We imagine them laughing disparagingly at any church 'trying to be cool' by embracing digital technology. Remember my taxi driver. Cringe.

Fear of the mockers, fear of the bemused, fear of the sceptical, fear of not being heard—fear of anything—is a bad basis for a decision. Don't base decisions about your church communications on fear of anyone or anything. The Bible says, in 2 Timothy 1:7, that we do *not* have a spirit of fear, but a spirit of power (enough to put our heads above the parapet), of love (enough to put concern into action), and of self-control (enough to see it through).

There will always be those who respond badly to anything that points to Christ and his church. As the early church was taught, 'The person without the Spirit does not accept the things that come from the Spirit of God but considers them foolishness' (1 Corinthians 2:14). However, 'God chose the foolish things of the world to shame the wise; God chose the weak things of the world to shame the strong' (1:27; read 1 Corinthians 1 and 2 to delve further into this topic).

Three opportunities

Here are three simple reasons churches can get excited about websites and know, without doubt, that the technology relates to them.

1. Because those unwilling to listen are online

Those who have already rejected Christianity are highly unlikely to be reached by traditional church. They are no more likely to come into church as a visitor on a Sunday morning than you are to stumble into a bookie's, or a strip club, or a playgroup, or whatever your equivalent of a no-go zone is. But the sceptical, the antagonistic and the anti-religious may spend the UK average of 20 hours on the internet each week.[3] This presents an amazing opportunity for those Christians who know how to use it wisely.

We know that the church isn't the building; it's the people. In the same way, the church online isn't the church website; it's the people of the church online, in whatever sphere, whether chatting on Facebook, responding to questions on email or offering advice on a forum. My husband heard from someone whose mission outreach was in a specialist online blogging community, contributing comments and bringing spiritual input into one particular community—in this case, focused on horror movies!

The internet provides the opportunity to bring spiritual content into *any* sphere. Things that, to some people, are insurmountable barriers to the gospel—church buildings and religious traditions— are removed. Contextual mission extends to relational networks between strangers, mediated by wi-fi.

Paul wrote:

Though I am free and belong to no one, I have made myself a slave to everyone, to win as many as possible… I have become all things to all people so that by all possible means I might save some. I do all this for the sake of the gospel, that I may share in its blessings. (1 Corinthians 9:19, 22b–23)

In November 2013 the Church of England set up a Task Group for Evangelism, bringing together a broad collection of people who were active in evangelistic ministry. The archbishops wrote:

Evangelism… can only be undertaken because God is alive and actively working by the Holy Spirit in families, parishes, places of work and everyday lives. The first movement is never from us to God, but always from God to us.[4]

So, if God is working in families, in places of work and in everyday lives, as the church we need to encourage a mission mindset everywhere, whether face to face or on the internet. New initiatives in online evangelism spring up all the time. The Church of England and many other denominations are investing in them. I can't wait to see what emerges.

2. Because church websites help us reach the willing

If you are one of those who are willing seriously to engage in digital communication—even if without much enthusiasm—perhaps you can identify with your friends who are willing (though not in a particularly proactive way) to entertain the idea of a God who communicates.

There are more than 10,000 baby christenings in the UK every month.[5] How many of these are families who are attempting to 'get the religion thing covered'—a neat one-hit social moment negating all guilt, satisfying the grandparents and bagging potentially useful godparents and school links at the same time?

This sounds cynical, but it's not. Friends who are at this stage of life are very willing to form a church connection when their children are small; it's like forming a strategic alliance in case it's needed for the future. The Church of England has set up a support hub to help the church make the most of this opportunity. And it shouldn't surprise us that the arrival of a baby—a searing reminder, loud, stretching and humbling—should be the time when ears once closed are forced open, and newly bemused parents find themselves perhaps even *willing* to (whisper whisper) consider going to church.

I really didn't think anyone still did the whole church on Sunday thing (this is not meant rudely, am just genuinely amazed)… Why do you go? Don't you want to have a lie-in with the papers?

This was the question thrown out publicly on a Wednesday afternoon in 2012 by one new mum, on the online forum Mumsnet.[6] It started a conversation—anonymous, candid, theological— with over 600 comments in six days. Here are some of the comments made possible by the forum:

I am totally into the God thing but find the whole church culture… middle class, patronising, sort of bristling with religion, all those shoulds and oughts, straining at gnats and missing elephants by a cubic mile. Uh oh, sounding judgmental (probably am).

I'd be interested to know why non-religious people describe themselves as freethinkers. I consider myself to be a freethinker too. I just happen to have decided that Christianity is true.

I think many in the West ignore their spiritual side.

It is good to be away from consumerism for an hour a week.

As a non-believer I often wish there was an equivalent of church:

1. *Church forces you to have some time for quiet contemplation.*
2. *There are often uplifting speakers who talk about their experiences of life and make you consider things from another's point of view.*
3. *You all have a good old sing-song which is very cathartic.*
4. *It brings people together as a village/community and fosters friendships that wouldn't come about under any other circumstances, typically between people of different ages, classes etc, all chatting together outside.*
5. *You feel really good afterwards.*

This conversation is a treasure trove of insight into the perspective of those sporadically sitting in pews who are not quite sure how they got there or why they keep coming back.

Perhaps it was the lack of guile in the original question that invited such a response. Perhaps it was the protection afforded by anonymity, or the chance for others to pile in with their own questions, possibly long suppressed: 'If you're a Christian, how did you get into it?' 'Do you really think…?'

A pastor of a number of smaller churches told me:

One of the hardest things I find in outreach is that it's incredibly difficult these days to meet people. Most people are either inside (home/car/work/ supermarket) or on the way somewhere. There is more anonymity, fewer encounters with strangers or half-acquaintances. To get into a conversation is very hard. We have forgotten how to initiate a conversation. Once you do, people are frequently open to talk.

We rely on courses like Alpha, Christianity Explored and Faith Pictures in our outreach because we need help to initiate the conversation. The fact is that it's hard to imagine such an intense, wide-ranging and open conversation as the one on Mumsnet happening among strangers in even the very best village pub. The many Christians who waded in to explain their faith did so eloquently, to those who really wanted to hear, all because a website created the space for the conversation to come up.

Recent research shows that 40% of those who have a Christian upbringing lose that identity later,[7] but 11% say they are 'spiritual'. Steve Aisthorpe's research into the 'Invisible Church'[8] helpfully sheds light on the large numbers who leave the church or are simply not able to attend on a Sunday morning, but still consider their faith to be strong. Most of those interviewed in his research had developed informal groups with Christian fellowship at the centre—'and several mentioned how the Internet had aided this'.[9]

One thing you can be sure about: for the majority of the 'willing', the internet is the first place they will look if…

- they are exploring Christianity outside of a traditional church.
- they are considering going to church for the first time.

Some may even seek to go to church online. Some physical churches show their services on the internet and invite comments while they take place, with responses and prayers. The Church of England is one organisation that has enabled this practice, with ChurchLive.[10]

This isn't the place to explore the theological questions raised by online church, fascinating though they are. If a church only exists online, is it really 'church'? Is it sufficiently incarnational and sacramental? Those involved would dispute the line sometimes drawn between an 'offline' and 'online' life. They are seeking to remove barriers of time, location and physical access.

Whatever the form, it is clear that church websites and online communities are able to reach those who are willing to engage, sometimes more quickly and effectively than if they were based in a building. If we want our voice to be heard, we need to be present in this space.

3. Because church websites help the curious to reach us

The 'curious' are the ones most likely to be already connected—on the fringe, friends with someone at the church, with a personal faith or perhaps not. They're actually reaching out to churches. In marketing parlance, they are the 'low-hanging fruit' (horrible phrase, I know), the ones most likely to notice any shift in your visual or online presence. They skim the church magazine and are most likely to come to your candlelight carol service or Easter egg hunt.

A church's digital presence is unlikely to be the basis for friendships (although that is possible), but it can enable and facilitate friend-making, providing a way in, a point of both discussion and connection. The book *Church Marketing 101*, written to help US churches, describes this intentional role of connecting people as 'marketing': 'At the very core of marketing is the connection of people to an entity—and there are no entities more worthy of time, money and effort than the body of Christ and Christ himself.'[11]

The word 'marketing' can create huge unease in churches. To some, it sounds like selling, associated with artifice, false promises or manipulation. But is this fair? There have been advertising campaigns with flawed motivations, even from within the church, which have tarnished the concept for some people. But marketing insights are essentially about communication skills. They can help churches create a digital presence which can even be a gateway to connection with God himself.

Thankfully, the website itself doesn't need to be divine. It just needs to make it easier for those who are already interested to connect with us.

Eight reasons people don't bother

We've looked at three reasons why church websites matter, based on the kind of people who will encounter them. Even so, people can build a case not to bother with them.

'Our website is perfect and I'm completely happy with it…' said no one, ever.

Our expectations of what a website can do are defined by the most famous and well resourced. Amazon can tell you what you want before you know yourself, and can deliver it tomorrow, raising the bar impossibly high for other companies to bear. BBC iPlayer is so intuitive that it can be navigated by a three-year-old, as many three-year-olds will happily demonstrate; therefore, no one expects to use more than the magic number of 'three clicks' to get to where they want. New visitors visit an average of 2.5 pages.

People are like sharks online: they search and consume. Our expectations of visual quality and design, raised by the sheer quantity of professional advertising around us, has made us more judgemental than we realise. Recent research in the US found that 47% of visitors will immediately disregard a church if the website design is poor.[12]

Faced with this pressure, many churches will retreat and fail to engage at all. The vision for why it matters will get lost.

So here are eight reasons why people don't bother with a church website.

1. Too complicated?

It can be; it doesn't need to be. The most complicated way is to do what one church did, and send Pam from the church office on an HTML course, in the hope that she'd transform from someone with little interest in digital communication to a design and technical genius. This is a shortcut to inflated expectation and frustration, or, as they'd say on Twitter, #fail.

It's as complicated as you make it. Chapter 3 shows ways to make it relatively simple.

Perhaps, though, 'It's too complicated' really means 'I don't want to have the awkward conversation with the guy who's doing it now.' This is tough. The stakes are high. If you can speak the truth in love, as the Bible teaches us to do, the most intractable volunteer may be persuaded of the benefits of sharing, or even releasing, control and power masquerading as responsibility.

2. Too exposing?

This can be a real concern for church leaders particularly in relation to social media: 'I already know plenty about the quirks and foibles of my congregation without seeing pictures of them on Facebook.' Fear of what you might see or say is high. Perhaps there's a fear of simply being seen.

The reality is that whether or not your church has a social media presence, people in your church may well be there already. If you address this reality in your teaching, you can help them shine their light more brightly in that context.

Other churches would say, 'We're a small community; we don't need a website that's open to the world.' But, as we've seen, the world is full of people who are very open to the possibility of a friendly, welcoming church. This is one way of showing them—of not hiding your light, but letting it shine.

3. We're too old to learn?

Internet usage among those aged 75+ is double what it was five years ago, at around 40%. The age group most likely to be increasing their use of the Internet is those aged 65–74.[13]

True, you'll probably always know less than the nearest eight-year-old. That's humbling, but no more so than going to another country and not being able to speak the language.

But don't make assumptions. My friend Veda was given an iPad for her 90th birthday and finds it very handy for emailing and video-calling distant relatives. In a doctoral thesis on church websites, Revd Dr Sara Batts suggested three ways churches could support older people getting online:

1. *Promote your church website as a safe place where people can start to engage with the internet and understand its uses and limitations without the risk of accidentally seeing illegal or disturbing content.*

2. *Encourage peer learning, teaching new skills within the congregation or community.*

3. *Make your site easy to navigate.*[14]

St John's Meads in Eastbourne set up a computer clinic in the parish hall as part of their weekly coffee morning. What a great idea!

There's that old saying: 'God doesn't call the equipped; he equips the called.' If there's no one else to do it, you can use the advice in this book, which is free from tech jargon.

One of the sad things about getting older is that there are fewer new skills to learn—but technology provides endless opportunity for new skills. It may take more determination, but it's possible. An effort to learn will be good for the brain, and, who knows, may unlock other skills or interests too.

4. Too much hard work?

Many worthwhile things are done by people who are tired and don't feel like doing them—and learning about websites is worthwhile.

A simple, up-to-date website is your church's shop window. Do you really want people to look for you online and find nothing, or just a few cobwebs? It's about stepping out of our building and facing our neighbours. It's about being found. It's about finding others, and showing them how to be found by God, in a way that doesn't depend on our availability.

If you put the work in now, perhaps someone considering using your church hall will find you online, discover a living body of Christ in their neighbourhood, look into what it means to be a Christian, and encounter God—even when your whole church leadership team are fast asleep in their beds.

5. Too unnecessary?

Joan: 'Everyone in our congregation is over 60. Our neighbours are mostly retired. We don't do email or mobiles, or anything like that. We're happy with a news sheet, noticeboard and magazine. That's enough.'

This will be the reality for many churches. In fact, half of the congregations of the UK Anglican Church are predominantly aged over 60, with fewer than five young people.

If that's you, keep your printed material. It matters. Add on something very simple (next steps in Chapter 3) and play your part in holding out a beacon of light. Play your part in showing the world that the church isn't dead. Maybe it will help give your own church a future.

There is nothing inherently bad about the internet, just as there is nothing bad about the concept of newspapers or phones or any other medium. It's possible to use it badly, but, if you use it well, it's a force for good. Small churches can see their networks increased, connecting with people of different ages and backgrounds.

If you still struggle to see the point, think of a website as a basic introduction/recommendation service, as low-maintenance as you need, but too good an option to dismiss altogether. If you have theological questions, by all means take the time to explore them[15] while moving forward as a church.

6. Too expensive?

This is a real concern, but sometimes based on misconception. A simple Facebook page or email address is free. A listing in one of the three main church directories is either free or very low cost. A basic website based on a template designed for churches can work out at around £20 a month over a year, including full support.[16] But this isn't really what I want to say. What I want to say is this: how we view church finances is about our perception of value.

- A cost of £200 a year is 55p a day, less than a bus fare or a newspaper. It's less than many churches spend on flowers, coffee or cleaning equipment.

- Money spent on a church website doesn't belong in the administration budget. It belongs in the evangelism budget. It is outreach, pure and simple. It's not for our benefit. It's for the benefit of those we're called and mandated to reach. It's one of the crucial ways that the poor know we care, and the curious know that God cares. It's part of having our feet fitted with the readiness of the gospel.
- It's not in the same category as buying staples or printer cartridges (one great joy of digital communication: no printer cartridges!). It's in the same category as inviting people to carols at Christmas, or producing posters for the notice-board or a magazine for the parish.
- It is better to give than receive.
- As any growing church will attest, funds invested in growth are fruitful far beyond any initial investments, perhaps in ways 'more than we can ask or imagine'. Take the long view.

Gordon Thorn spends all week talking to churches about their websites, for Church123. This is what he told me:

Churches do need to save money, but investing in the right places will bring fruit. I suspect there is a very direct link between churches that do not invest online and the ones that are sadly reducing and eventually closing down. Spending thousands a year [on a website] for many churches would be a waste of money when they could spend a few hundred and get the same fruit.

7. Too time-consuming?

Aaaah—this is the crux.

I get it. I really do. My husband is a church leader. Sometimes people ask me if that means he only works one day a week—cue a slightly hollow laugh. It can be hard to imagine prioritising anything new.

At CPO (Christian Publishing & Outreach) we hear from churches where the members' meeting or Parish Church Council has such a long agenda that anything to do with our great commission (including church communication, welcome, outreach and mission) is regularly neglected. The necessities of caring for the congregation take priority (including really exciting things like insurance, fixing the broken tiles, rotas and so on).

How did our priorities get so skewed? It's not enough to write a Mission Action Plan. Its value is entirely in the way the plan is put into practice, even if there are multiple setbacks and failures along the way.

The next chapter will show how it is possible, with the right planning, to set up a small project, with a small team and a small initial investment. There will be defined delegated responsibility and a simple line of accountability. It's a step—and, as on any journey, it's just one step after another. Not so overwhelming: just do the next thing.

8. Too hard to sustain?

It is very true that if you establish a whole new habit out of nowhere, it is unlikely to survive the inevitable death of initial enthusiasm. The keen volunteer leaves. Updating gets forgotten.

This is no excuse not to bother, because…

- you can enter an 'expiration date' for any online content, when it will automatically disappear— planned obsolescence, if you like.
- you can plan a good strategy around your capacity, and around workable techniques of habit creation (see Chapter 2).

Here's the summary of why it matters

- If our church is invisible online, those searching will assume it has closed down. We can expect very few visitors.
- If our church is listed in an online directory, but with no website, we don't get the opportunity to show the full picture of all we are and all we do.
- If we have a website but it's woefully out of date, it looks as if we don't care, or stopped putting on events at Easter 2014. If a church neglects its communication, does it also neglect its people? Is it a neglectful church?
- If our website is up to date but talks only about our buildings and activities, not about our people, our beliefs, our God or the hope that we have in Christ—and doesn't enable people to see a route to discovering more about these things—do we inadvertently communicate that the church, rather than Christ, is the end point? Do we set ourselves up to be the solution to people's problems, rather than pointing to the grace on which we rely?

In case you're feeling got at—*choose conviction, not accusation!*

It's easy to feel guilty. We feel the accusation of those outside the church: 'You're so behind the times.' We may even feel an accusation from this book: 'You should be doing more.'

First, the fact that you picked the book up and have read this far shows that you're doing more than you realise. There's no condemnation here. Those who are serving tirelessly in churches to serve their community and God deserve support and respect, not further demands. It's not that you *should* be doing more—it's that you *can* take the next step with vision, motivation, purpose, even excitement.

The Bible describes the devil as an enemy who 'accuses… day and night' (Revelation 12:10). Accusation leads to defensiveness and passivity—not to action. It's not the voice of God.

One of the most liberating truths I was ever taught was the difference between conviction and condemnation. 'There is now *no condemnation* for those who are in Christ Jesus' (Romans 8:1). When I feel condemned, it's not from God. When I feel convicted, however, it can be the power of the Holy Spirit, calling me to action and probably to repentance. 'Dear children, let us not love with words or speech but with actions and in truth,' says 1 John 3:18.

When we communicate as a church, in action, in truth, it is an act of love.

In one of his last pieces of public communication before he officially retired, Pope Benedict XVI put it this way:

The digital environment is not a parallel or purely virtual world, but is part of the daily experience of many people, especially the young. Social networks are the result of human interaction, but for their part they also reshape the dynamics of communication which builds relationships: a considered understanding of this environment is therefore a prerequisite for a significant presence there.[17]

Imagine this...

Max has walked past your church every day. He's never knowingly met a 'card-carrying Christian', the type who goes to church, prays or reads the Bible, and he's only been to church for a wedding. But one night after a rubbish day at work he realises he needs community. He's googling his neighbourhood. He is astonished the church has a website. Clean, straightforward, answering every question he would have asked about what goes on, who is there, why they do what they do. This is a church that confounds all his stereotypes, drives him deeper into searches for long-buried questions about spirituality, increases his curiosity and points him to people who can help. Who knows, he may even poke his nose round the door one day.

The Watsons have just moved in up the road. They knew within a week that yours is a community church, not the stuffy, pious kind of their childhoods. They see evidence of connections with the school, and of activities designed to help the most poor and needy in society and the world. This appeals to them. They haven't met anyone from the church yet, but everything they've found online about the church has stacked up with what they've seen. They get the sense they'd be welcome. Now it's just a matter of finding a free Sunday morning… they might email the vicar first.

The fight for people's attention grows.

You don't need to do much to stay in the sight lines of those looking for you. What you *can't* do is be invisible.

It doesn't take much—not really. Not in the context of a year. Not in the light of eternity.

All you need is a plan.

2

What to consider first

The Church of England project Evidence to Action concluded that churches that grow are 'intentional about vision and strategy', and 'recognise the importance of a clear identity and not neglecting the spiritual health of the church'.[18] The strategy is where the church leadership should be closely involved, and then they may hand it on to others.

Before you set out to create or overhaul your church plan for websites and digital communication, there are six strategic questions which can form the foundation of a long-term plan. Take these questions and discuss them with a group.

- What is our current reality?
- Who is our focus?
- What is the core message we're communicating?
- What is our approach to social media?
- Can we communicate an identity that is cohesive, consistent and credible?
- Are our expectations realistic and shared with the church?

What is our current reality?

Some church strategies use the simple framework: what is, what could be, what will be? Here are some questions to get you started.[19]

1 Are we registered on any directories, for example, 'Find a Church'?
2 How would we describe the people most likely to be looking at our website? What do we know about them?
3 What budget could be released? In one amount or monthly?
4 If we have a website, do we really know how to edit it, how it is supported, and who is responsible for every aspect of its content?
5 Have we looked at every page with a pen in hand?
6 Is there anything on there which is out of date? If so, do we know why? What would we do to avoid this next time?
7 Do we feel that our website reflects our values and priorities as a church?
8 Look at the website from the perspective of a local person who has never been to church and never met a Christian. Is it easy to find out when we meet, who we are, what we believe and what's going on?

9 If we had to justify why we're putting effort into this, what would be our answer?

Hopefully you'll now know enough for a basic SWOT analysis:

- Strengths: what we want to keep
- Weaknesses: what makes us cringe (or sometimes, what makes us disagree)
- Opportunities: what we want to develop
- Threats: what could go horribly wrong, probably by accident

Ultimately the answer to the last question is key. The motivation, the vision, the 'why it matters' covered in Chapter 1, is the engine that will keep you going through the minutiae of planning.

Digital tools will never be more than part of the bigger picture of the whole of your church communication: the preaching, magazine, smiles, welcome, noticeboard, invitations, activities, publicity, and everything else.

Jesus said that his followers would be identified by their love for one another (John 13:35). When we use church communications to build community, it enables that community to grow in love, which in turn enables us to communicate better.

In 2001 Jim Collins wrote a seminal management book called *Good to Great*, which was later appropriated for churches in *Breakout Churches* by Thom Rainer. Rainer observed this:

Breakout churches are not adverse [sic] to innovation… Once they accepted a new approach, they were quick to use it for the good of the church. They viewed innovation as an acceleration of growth, not a creator of growth.[20]

In other words, first identify where you want to develop, and then use digital tools to support your development. If you ask UK churches what type of people they want to attract, most will answer, 'Young families'—and for good reason. Churches with young people are twice as likely to be flourishing.[21] Don't think that setting up a website aimed at young families is enough. It needs to support what is already taking root. Even just the process of planning your strategy may improve your communication internally, and therefore improve your outreach.

Who is our focus?

Marketing organisations build 'personas' of target customers or donors, to hone their advertising. Recent research on 'why Christians give' presented a persona of a typical Christian donor: '55–64, male, graduate, married, in full-time employment, in household with pretax income £30–40k, with active role in local church'.[22]

Building a 'persona' of the local person you have in mind may actually help as you think through your strategy. The members of one church I know keep in mind their fictitious guy in his late 20s who enjoys live music and probably has a tattoo. In my role at CPO, when we develop designs, I keep in mind particular churches I've visited. Would this work in their context? Could it succeed in appealing both to the church and to those they're trying to reach?

Obviously, it's God who is the ultimate communicator, and he is already at work in the church and the community. We look for where God is at work and join him in it. The point is this: all strategy needs to begin with *who*.

In churches there are 'gatekeepers'—people who, if won round, open the way for everyone else to follow. The voice of church members will always be the loudest there. There isn't a representative of your non-believing neighbours in your meetings. Yet they are the ultimate audience for your church website. How can you hear their voice? Here are some ideas.

Use the tools listed in Chapter 4 (under 'To build a picture of your neighbourhood') to find data about your local community.

If you're feeling brave, supplement this information by using a story in the local newspaper, an online survey or a questionnaire at a local community group to find out what neighbours think of your church and how you can serve them. (There is more about this in *Church from the Outside* in this series.)

A new parent in the area, looking for groups to join, will probably go to a local online directory or blog for advice. The youth service social media will be a better way to advertise your youth group than a poster.

One London church was aware of high levels of family breakdown in their area. They put on a marriage course and advertised it using Google AdWords.[23] The keywords? 'Divorce lawyer near me'.

Research has shown that the church is dispro-portionately well educated, but this doesn't mean we're better at communicating clearly. If local people speak English as an additional language, consider giving information in multiple languages. Simple language will reach more people.

Where possible, ask for people's communication preferences. Perhaps they would prefer a text to email. Apart from being polite to ask, it's now acknowledged in marketing and fundraising that people are more likely to respond if they are in control of the way they're contacted. Generational differences are reflected in communication preferences—and yet, as Martyn Payne has explored for Messy Church, churches are called to be inherently intergenerational, places where all ages relate as fellow children of God.[24] No communication stream should be restricted to a particular age group.

So make it a habit to ask new people how they'd prefer to be contacted. If you can capture this on a database, even better.

Go through each existing group, activity or ministry in your church, to see if you can identify the best way to communicate with them centrally and the best way for them to communicate with each other. See where you can bring digital tools into this mix, to supplement, hopefully even replace, default 'notices' from the front on a Sunday. Finally, ensure you always have an opt-out on every form of communication. Data protection within churches is really important. You should find up-to-date advice from the church online administration providers listed in Chapter 4 (Toolkit).

Now, talk about the people you want to reach. Where are they online? Can people in the congregation join them there?

The target audience is likely to be:

- The local 'curious' (see Chapter 1) who don't go to church
- The existing congregation
- Christians moving to the area
- People looking for venue hire or groups meeting in the church

There are other specialist audiences—including perhaps historians if yours is an old building—but these four are the main ones, and this priority order makes sense for most churches.

What is the core message we're communicating?

Now that you've thought through your focus, this will be the lens through which you'll view each digital tool. Other books in this series look more closely at internal communication and social media, and how some of these tools work best when they're linked closely to existing print and spoken communications. For example, could you use print to publicise your website?

Here are some brief examples of core messages and functions for various digital tools, and how they may be used differently if they're focused internally (In) or externally (Out).

Websites

- In: a 'login' area for rotas and so on, or a spring-board to online social networks—for example, for prayer requests.[25]
- Out: an introduction to church activities, people, and the Christian faith

Apps (shown as icons on a smartphone)

- In: logging children into Sunday groups. Apps are best when they perform a function that a website cannot. Augmented reality apps like Blippar, which superimpose virtual images over real ones, will present huge opportunities for churches in the future, particularly tourist churches.
- Out: talks—but a podcast (publicly available for people to subscribe to) may be enough.

Blog (series of articles) or vlog (video blog)

- In: church news, book reviews, pastoral reflections, group meetings over social media or Skype (free internet video and voice calls), training sessions or conferences.
- Out: thoughts from a church leader, news on events past and future, testimonies, stories from people connected to church, welcome video, clips from YouTube in services.

Email

- In: weekly central update. (It is a legal requirement that people can unsubscribe easily.)
- Out: relevant updates to those who've signed up for news

Text

- In: the most effective reminder method of all
- Out: not advisable

When you're considering which tool is best for which audience, think about how Jesus contextualised his communication for his audience. He knew whether each person was preoccupied with sheep or corn or religion, and he met them at that point.

He knew how to tell a story that suited the context, whether it was a crowd or an intimate gathering. We have so much to learn from him as we explore sharing our faith with a greater range of tools at our disposal than ever before.

What is our approach to social media?

There is an increasing level of support for UK churches in social media. Chapter 4 (Toolkit) suggests ways to stay informed. If you're talking about websites, you'll end up talking about social media, and this is necessary.

Social media can reach places others can't reach, providing the opportunity to share, to listen, to create conversation, to find common ground. It becomes possible to participate in the practices of church—to learn, meet others, and grow spiritually—beyond geographical or physical limitations. Fads like the 'Pokemon Go' game showed how churches can literally have people arriving at the door, led there by digital community.[26]

If you have social media, include clear links to it on your website. If social media seems outside or beyond your current situation, you still need to understand how it works. You still need to read up. Your approach might not be to set up a Facebook and Twitter church presence—but at least it should be to stay informed.

Like anything ubiquitous and culture-shifting, social media needs to be recognised and talked about in any church that is serious about reaching its community. The *Social Media* book in this series addresses the practicalities, guidelines and questions on this more fully.

Can we communicate an identity that is cohesive, consistent and credible?

Church communication in any form is trying to broker a relationship between an individual and an organisation. Ultimately, of course, it's trying to point beyond the organisational façade to a group of similar people, and a God who is interested in long-term relationship, with an eternal legacy.

'Relational marketing' is the term used for a marketing situation where every point of contact is viewed in the context of a long-term relationship, or 'brand loyalty'. Fundraisers will talk about the 'lifetime value' of a donor, valuing long-term faithfulness over short-term generosity. Churches wouldn't use the phrase 'relational marketing' to describe outreach, but perhaps there are lessons from 'relational marketers' that we can learn. Without being deterred by the language, see if you can see any helpful parallels.

People are becoming extremely savvy at evaluating the positioning of any company from even the briefest glance at a website. As one writer puts it:

Internet presence has become the primary way people evaluate churches—which means they evaluate all churches, even if they only visit one. Websites are seldom read, but they are always evaluated.[27]

There are two questions behind the evaluation:

- Does this look like 'my kind of place'?
- Will I be able to find what I'm looking for?

These are the same questions people ask when they turn up at the church door. We all seek signs of cohesion, of consistency, of credibility. If the website is the first place where people have encountered the church, they will be looking for signs of internal consistency. 'Is this what I have been led to expect?'

As Christian thinker and researcher on social media Dr Bex Lewis puts it: 'Visitors should not be shocked by a disconnect between what is "advertised" and what they experience.'[28]

Marketers use this mantra: 'Attract—Convert—Close —Delight'. In e-commerce it charts a progression: a target customer is first attracted to a website or place, then 'converted' by a call to action (like signing up to a newsletter or sharing their details). 'Close' means that they buy something, possibly even coming back for more or becoming a repeat visitor. Hopefully they will have enough 'delight' in the experience to become a 'brand promoter', recommending you to others. This is the ultimate aim.

The aim of customer service teams, brilliantly, is to delight you, even if it's through automated tools. They'd bring round a cup of tea in person if they could. The equivalent for churches is the welcome. You can have the best website in the world, but a grumpy reception will entirely undermine it. (There's more on this in *Church from the Outside,* in this series.)

Churches are not trying to push people through a process. We all know it's far messier than that. In the parable of the sower, Jesus punctured any notion that all the 'seeds we sow' will produce grain—or that we can control the way things turn out (Matthew 13:3–8, 18–23). Certainly, not everyone we attract will go on to 'multiply'.

Our website can be part of the 'attract' stage, or the sowing. Some people may meet us as a result of it, whether on a Sunday, at an event, or perhaps online. For them to do this, though, there will need to be a 'call to action': 'Come along, you're always welcome'; 'Email your prayer request'; 'Watch the service online'; 'Sign up for more information'.

The progression from 'Convert' to 'Close' to 'Delight' is not achievable with digital tools alone. It is about a genuine welcome, appropriate follow-up (using people's stated communication preference), and the offer of friendship and discipleship.

This is why it makes a difference when all forms of your church communication—your posters, magazine, noticeboards, website and social media headers if you have them—look the same. Corporate brands know that people join the dots, and what that want people to see is a group who know who they are and what they're doing. Consistency creates coherence—and coherence helps credibility.

This is what branding means. Branding is not about having a professionally designed logo, although sometimes that may be necessary. It's about having a consistent, coherent, credible identity, with some kind of recognisable visual representation.

The next chapter suggests ways you can make your communication look consistent, perhaps with a logo and favourite colours and fonts. Even if your website has been written by ten different people, it needs to speak with one voice—one clear, jargon-free, punchy voice.

Are our expectations realistic and shared with the church?

A strategy requires buy-in. Enough people need to be behind the general direction, even if they're clueless about the detail. Good internal communication makes external communication easier.

It's not enough to paint a vision of how wonderful things could be. Motivation to change also requires dissatisfaction with the present.

I was on holiday recently. My children made some friends on the beach, who invited them to a family movie in the church on Friday afternoon. Brilliant idea—use the church screens as a community family cinema outreach! I made a note to look up the time online, but all I could find was a listing in a community site from two summers ago (probably when it started and they were more publicity-keen). There was no church website and it wasn't office hours so I couldn't call to ask. Funnily enough, we didn't go.

If your church doesn't have a website, tell stories like this. 'Think of all the opportunities we're missing!' Talk through the 'reasons not to bother' in Chapter 1. Then explain that a website won't solve all the problems or instantly yield results—but it is the necessary next step.

Realistic shared expectations will require a joint effort. Your digital communications must be part of your overall church communication strategy. They can't stand alone. The people responsible for every format—magazines, noticeboards, posters, website, any social media, events and talks—will all benefit from a regular conversation to plan and to ensure that everything matches as closely as possible.

One person who is passionate about banning typos and grammatical errors might be willing to do this for every communication type. Another person with a real eye for graphic design can ensure that standards are high across the board.

Here are some ways to find hidden people who care. Look for…

- those most involved in the local community, who are able to see what you do from the perspective of their neighbours.
- one of their friends, who can assess your website as an 'outsider'.
- anyone passionate about contextual mission or outreach.
- people who enthuse about new technology.
- anyone who takes up a public opportunity to express opinions on the magazine or to do training on a tool like Publisher.
- artists; avid exhibition-goers; people with graphic design on their walls at home, and opinions about fonts.
- anyone who enters a competition to design a poster or magazine for Easter: creating designs for Easter isn't easy.
- anyone who's taken the initiative to improve communication for their ministry, group or club.
- a church leader who is committed to growing the church.

Notice that I haven't said you should jump on a website coder or journalist or self-proclaimed 'expert'. They don't always have the skills needed for improving or starting a church website, because the technology of a website isn't the same as its purpose, and writing for print isn't the same as effective digital communication.

Churches can experience the stop-and-start process in their communications—the difference between ongoing 'maintenance mode' and exciting 'baseline progress'. I've come to think of it as a helpful plateau principle. It goes like this.

Someone with energy and motivation notices something that could be better, and initiates change. This might involve training or money or both. There's a noticeable improvement. Everyone breathes a sigh of relief. Then you hit a plateau. Everyone takes their eye off the ball, and, until someone else with energy and motivation notices… You get the idea.

The trick is to make enough improvement to allow for the plateau. Your team need to know that the levels of energy when you begin the project don't need to continue at that pitch for ever. See how much progress can be made while you're focused, and you may even find that it carries you for a while.

Even after all that initial energy, you'll still need some sustainability to keep your website up to date.

In the book *The Power of Habit*,[29] Charles Duhigg uses many case studies to show the three things needed to establish a new habit: a trigger, a routine and a reward. This can be a really helpful principle for integrating digital communications into your existing patterns.

A trigger for updating a church website might be the production of a weekly news sheet. It has to be something you already do, a habit which is already ingrained.

The routine might be a list of pages to check. Over time, it becomes almost automatic.

The reward might be the satisfaction of telling someone 'We've done it,' or a check to see how many people have visited the site this week. (Your website provider may tell you this, or you could sign up to Google Analytics for a report with far more information than you'll need, but enough to show you it's all worthwhile.[30]) Or maybe your reward could just be a slice of cake.

Hopefully you'll have a strategy team in place before you dive into the planning in the next chapter.

3

Essential next steps

There may be whole sections of this next chapter that you skip. Choose what is relevant to you. New digital tools appear all the time, so treat this as a starter.

Before looking at websites, a word about email, text and event planning. If you have a website, you'll probably be sending out regular emails. Tools like Mailchimp and Dotmailer will enable you to add images using templates, and allow people to unsubscribe easily. Larger churches, for example, could have one list for regular members, and another for those who've made contact but are less connected. See it as a digital version of a parish magazine.

For graphic ('HTML') emails, a logo at the top left and a title may be enough. You can create a graphic header incorporating your logo, using an online graphics tool, or take a photo yourself and crop it to the right dimensions. Even in a normal email you can create a signature, using a small logo and basic contact information.

For event planning you can use tools like Eventbrite to take booking details and payment. For rota planning and calendars, try Doodle to find a mutually convenient date (free and very simple), and Google Calendar for something everyone can see. To collect feedback, a free tool like Survey Monkey can give you valuable information that you may never hear in person. Used carefully, it's powerful.

If you have sufficient funds for a monthly budget, speak to church administration experts like those listed in Chapter 4 (Toolkit). You'll also find places to go for excellent advice on online fundraising, which can transform giving and appeals for churches.

A good church email should link to places for further information—for example, a website, a talk online, a support organisation, an email address or a place to sign up. The 'call to action' is where digital communication can achieve a better response than print or spoken word: 'Sign up here'; 'Email to tell us what you think'; 'Fill in this quick survey'.

An email can also reinforce messages from other places, informing people about what's going on and reminding them of the vision behind it. Try to create structure and regularity to make it easier to plan. A simple template with gaps to fill will really help a time-starved volunteer—and you can always intersperse the regular weekly or monthly email with something a little more fun: 'A personal note from the vicar'.

Now for a website plan. All you need to do is choose your tool, choose your look, plan your menu, plan your content, and be visible. Easy! At each stage, take what is most relevant to your situation. And remember, it doesn't need to be perfect, but it does need to be up to date.

Choose your tool

If you don't have one already, you'll need a domain name (for example, myvillagechurch.org.uk). If you use a church website provider, they'll sort it out for you.

This is not the place to be creative! The more obvious and boring the name is, the easier it will be for people to find you. The ending .org shows that you are a charity rather than a company. Include your village or town in the address if you have a common church name.

You should expect to have email addresses that match your domain—for example, children@myvillagechurch.org.uk / MikeB@myvillagechurch.org.uk. This is immensely reassuring for people contacting you and enables you to set up appropriate emails quickly for different people, teams or even events. You could assign 'bookings@myvillagechurch.org.uk' to whoever is responsible for venue hire. This is a simple professional approach.

Although Gmail, Hotmail and Yahoo emails are wonderful (and free), they are designed for personal use and will look too informal for an organisation. There are some helpful tips on email addresses and avoiding spam at www.church123.com/church_email_addresses.

Here's your very quick guide to some web design vocab, so that you can throw in the occasional acronym and sound like an expert—or at least like someone who won't get fobbed off. It's a game of 'spot the jargon'. Ready?

'Front-end' web designers are primarily interested in the 'look and feel' of your website. They make sure it offers a really good 'user experience' (or 'UX' for short). They talk about things like 'information architecture' (the way information is prioritised and arranged) and 'nice responsive UI' (a 'user interface' that changes in size, depending on whether you're using a mobile, tablet or computer).

'Back-end' developers—or coders—offer something different. They build the machinery behind the website, making it function like a well-oiled purring motorbike. Occasionally, but rarely, they're also good at design. They talk about things most people don't understand, like SQL databases, CSS and HTML. Sometimes they like to stay in a darkened room for a really long time to concentrate. There's a great organisation called Kingdom Code, whose members gather this expertise to discover ways to serve Jesus.

The best combination is when a designer has explained to a developer what is required, and they've worked together to produce a site with speed, power and style. This is what web agencies offer.

Increasingly, the 'back-end' coded bit is hidden behind templates or systems, so that someone with no technical expertise can create clever effects, using 'content management systems' (CMS). These can be built for you so that you can edit sites yourself, or some are available 'off the shelf'. Some (as you'll see below) are designed specifically for churches. We've called them 'click-and-build' systems.

Some template 'platforms', or systems, are publicly available—or 'open source'. Examples are Wordpress, Drupal, Wix and Squarespace. Some are very simple; others can be shaped and have 'modules' or 'widgits' added to build something incredibly sophisticated. You don't need to use all the capabilities to create something good.[31]

Some people think there are inherent security concerns with anything 'open source' and would rather create something 'bespoke'. I think it's fair to say that nowadays every system can be hacked. All we can do is take sensible precautions and require that anyone providing a website for us can explain how they've done the same.

Now that you're an expert, you have three options for building your site: a volunteer, a website agency, or a click-and-build system.

A volunteer

- Pros: cheap; probably someone you know.
- Cons: they may leave, they may run out of time, not many do it well, *and* it's probably someone you know…

There are five crucial questions to ask a volunteer web designer:

1. 'Can we see examples of other websites you've done?' (Translation: do you actually have a clue what you're doing?)

- Good answer: 'Yes, I help out a few other churches and charities. Have a look and tell me what you think.' *(Check that they really are open to feedback.)*
- Bad answer: 'I haven't got any online as such…' If this is their first website, do you really want the public face of your church to be a guinea pig project? No!

2. 'What platform would you use?' (Translation: are you going to set up our website using a system that other people can understand and edit, or do you want to make it yours and yours alone?)

- Good answer: 'Wordpress / Blogger / Squarespace or similar.'
- Bad answer: 'Bespoke / I'll just code it from scratch.'

3. 'Do you see yourself more as a developer or as a front-end website designer?' (Translation: is your priority making it look good or not? Do you understand that it needs to function both front and back?)

- Good answer: 'I'm most interested in how the website will be used.'
- Bad answer: 'I'm a really good coder, so everything's covered.'

4. 'How much time realistically are you able to give to this?' (Translation: are you going to overpromise and underdeliver? Will we still be patiently begging for progress in a year's time?)

- Good answer: 'Give me the content and we'll agree a date to review. After that I'll set aside a certain time each week / month, or train someone.'
- Bad answer: 'I love working at 3.00 am! I'll be fine! I'm sure!'

5. 'How do you think this could work long-term?' (Translation: are you going to move away and leave us in the lurch?)

- Good answer: 'My plan includes backups, security and full training on this system for others.'
- Bad answer: 'Hey, Jesus could come back tomorrow; let's not worry about that.'

The ideal church website volunteer—and there are many—is someone who has…

- professional up-to-date skills in web design, which they're willing to offer, perhaps to build up their portfolio.
- commitment to the church and its vision, good relationships with the team, an understanding of the church communication needs and a willingness to receive feedback positively.
- a plan for training others within the church once the initial site is set up.

Without all of this, be wary. Countless churches have entrusted the significant responsibility of representing their church to the world to someone who doesn't have time, doesn't know what they're doing or doesn't really care, or all three. You'll need a back-up plan in case they disappear.

A web design agency

- Pros: flexible; high-quality (hopefully)
- Cons: high initial cost; possible ongoing support costs; expensive to redesign

As well as the questions you'd ask a volunteer, also ask:

- What is the development process? Who will our main contact be?
- Do you offer any training on updating the site, adding images, adding new features and so on?
- What level of technical support can you offer? If we have a volunteer struggling to update a page, can you help? If we want a new email address, will this be an additional cost?
- Have you provided church websites before, or is there someone who can work with us who understands church requirements—and understands churches?
- What are the ongoing costs?

Consider too whether you feel an affinity with the company. Are they genuinely supportive of your vision?

Click-and-build websites (CMS)

- Pros: lots of options designed specifically for churches; easy to use—no technical knowledge needed; more potential for lots of people to edit and run. The tool should handle everything technical, which will save your church lots of time as you can just focus on what you want to say.
- Cons: may not be as flexible as a fully bespoke custom site.

UK church website providers have been set up precisely to do the hard work so that you don't have to. You can call their helpdesk and ask questions to a real person. If you have a positive initial conversation, and it sounds like a solution that would work, you not only end up with a great website, but you also get to support a ministry of providing websites to other churches too.

Here are ten questions to ask a church website provider.

1. 'Can I see examples of church websites that have used your tool?' A brave answer would be to show a bad example as well as a good one. The best editor in the world can still produce a really ugly website—because it's as much your responsibility as theirs.
2. 'Do you have a summary of all the features you offer?' There may only be small differences between providers, but remember to focus on what you are most likely to use. A large number of features may be totally irrelevant, so don't just pick a bigger feature list.
3. 'Can you transfer any existing domain name or content?' This option should be offered, but you

may need to provide details and work together if passwords have been lost or forgotten.

4. 'Can I have a free trial? What does it cost over a year?' You won't know how it works until you try.

5. 'Do you have options to upgrade in the future to a different template or bespoke site?' If you don't see templates or suggestions that suit you, explain what you want, with examples. Creative solutions may be possible—you don't know until you ask.

6. 'Can you help us access content from other organisations or resources?' There may be options to automatically create pages introducing Christianity or pages for well-known courses and so on.

7. 'What ongoing technical support do you offer?' There will be times when you just need someone at the end of the phone to talk it through.

8. 'Why would you recommend we use you rather than any other provider?' Every organisation has strengths: the best will recognise this and be able to answer the question from your perspective, not theirs. It's always encouraging when Christians are gracious towards their competitors, recognising that we are all working ultimately towards the same goal.

9.   'Do you understand my situation?' In other words—have you listened? Do you hear what I need? Do you 'get' my church?

10. 'Do you have a statement of faith as an organisation?' Believe it or not, this question isn't about doctrinal allegiance. It's simply checking whether an organisation purporting to serve the church is motivated by that aim, and not by making money out of churches to the detriment of other ministries. If you have the choice, choose those who are trying to build up the kingdom of God. Look for those who know what you're trying to say and the sensitivities that are unique to churches.

How you run your church website is an important but not a critical decision. In truth, any of these options could probably work.

If anything, it may be a decision where the timing (and possibly process) matters most. Just don't be one of those churches that never improve the situation because 'we're still trying to find the perfect solution'. Take a risk. Reach out. The outcome may be better than what you currently have, especially if you use the advice below!

Choose your look

If you're starting a church website from scratch, you already have plenty of visual material that defines your church 'look'. You have the congregation. Possibly a building. Definitely a local neighbourhood. Possibly some signs, posters, noticeboards or banners. You may have a church logo or a denominational logo. You also have an ethos or personality as a church, which fits more closely with some colours, fonts or images than others. A creative person could help you identify this.

Here are two examples:

- Grace Church Hackney, in London, has a larger proportion than most of hipster 20-somethings. Their website (www.gracechurchhackney.org.uk) has typewriter fonts, gritty urban photos, and lots of grey and bronze colours.
- St John's Meads in Eastbourne is also a Church of England congregation, with a mix of retired people and young families. Their website (www.stjm.org.uk) uses friendly handwriting fonts, photos of smiling faces, and lots of pale blue and yellow.

What these websites have in common is that they show internal consistency. They feel the same on every page. They both demonstrate communities who know who they are and what they stand for. You don't get the sense of a maverick individual volunteer 'webmaster' experimenting with ghastly fonts and animations.

Branding is more than just a logo. It's an attempt at a visual representation of values and ethos. One web developer sums it up like this: 'Your church is not a building, it's a community, and your website should be based around these real people, reflecting their real age, beauty and ethnicity in photos, design and content.'[32]

This is why a website can't be developed without some input from a church leadership team. If your church has a Mission Action Plan, a strategy or any kind of long-term plan, the website is part of it—even down to how it looks and the visual first impression that it gives of your church's character.

Other books in this series look at branding and logos in more depth, and there are some tools and links in Chapter 4 on choosing images for your site. For now, here are some basic tips.

- Use no more than two fonts.
- Church logo should probably be top left, denominational logo at the top or bottom.
- Avoid coloured text against coloured backgrounds.
- Use images that are optimised to the right size so that they don't take ages to load (see more in Chapter 4: Toolkit).
- Choose images that include people (but not children's faces, unless you have permission) and are a fair reflection of your church.
- Choose images you have permission to use.
- Say no to adverts.
- Avoid error pages by testing everything.

Your website may look different on different browsers (for example, Internet Explorer, Chrome, Safari or Firefox) and different again on different-sized screens (phone, tablets of various sizes, TV or PC). Good websites are 'responsive' to different sizes. (Ask your provider to test this.) Google Fonts are free and work on all browsers.

Plan your menu

Your menu needs to be led by the priorities of your audience. As the adman Steve Krug said, 'Don't make me think!' It needs to be intuitive.

People probably expect…

- a logo in the top left corner
- address / phone number / Registered Charity number at the very bottom
- 'Home' at the left-hand end of the main menu
- 'Contact' either at the right-hand end of the main menu or in the footer
- any social media icons—for example, Facebook and Twitter—top right or at the bottom
- service times on the home page.

People probably won't like…

- out-of-date content
- large, slow-to-load pictures
- an incomprehensible statement of belief
- spinning logos or music
- 'Page under construction'
- guestbooks or 'members only' barriers
- submenus more than two or three levels deep

When planning your menu, never lose sight of who the website is for. It's your main shop window. If you want people to stumble across the site via search engines, when looking for something else—local history, community groups or areas of interest, a big event, relationship advice or financial advice—you could create jargon-free 'bridge' pages to the main content.

Combining pages can work. For instance, 'Beliefs and history' could explain to architecture buffs the theological significance of your building and how it relates to your life today. 'Contact and directions' encourages people to visit as well as send you an email (you could go the extra mile and include details like bus routes).

Popular groups or activities could have their own page—which means that the person responsible can be in charge of keeping them up to date. Alternatively, put them all on one page as a way of showing the range of activities. It makes sense for the parent and toddler group information to be in the same place as something about Sunday activities or holiday clubs.

Your key menu headings will be as follows.

Home page

Include your service times, your location, the full name of your church and your denomination. This will help Google to find you.

Less is more. Short sentences. Short paragraphs.

Short! You've got five seconds max to get people's attention. Saying one thing well is better than saying ten things in a sea of wordy proclamations.

If you have an image or logo for an event or course, you can put it here, linking to the event's own page. Hopefully this will match any other printed publicity you've produced. CPO, for example, produce website templates and social media images to match some design ranges. When using seasonal templates, make sure they are for the current season: don't let your website be the ghost of Christmas past.

If you have an excellent social media stream, you could show it on the home page (your developers will insert it as a 'widgit'). Something current can be great, but only if it's sustainable and, well, current. A bad social media feed makes the homepage worse, not better.

If it is good, a short welcome video can work well. Don't make it play automatically—give people the choice—but you could produce a quick whizz around with a camera, a few shots of the church 'in action' with people, and a face saying 'hello'. It should probably last no more than 20 seconds. Give it a try just for fun, even if you don't use it. It will help you think about what you want to communicate. But don't use video just because you've spent time on it. Ask a friend who's not a Christian. If it puts them off, take it off.

One writer on the theology of digital communication suggests testing to see whether a new visitor can see the 'big idea' of your website in the time it takes to sing 'Happy Birthday'.[33] That's the length of time an average visitor will look at a website. Your home page is where they'll start. In that time, can you find what you want them to find?

Questions about Christianity / What we believe / Our vision

This page is for people who may not come to church on a Sunday, but are curious. You can link to sites like those listed in Chapter 4 (Toolkit), and give a statement of what you believe and why. Include some vision, but be wary of full doctrinal statements on these pages, which may be incomprehensible to visitors (or, let's face it, even to those in the church). If you're running a course for the curious, link to it here.

Who we are / Who's who / About us

Churches sometimes include these elements either on one page or a submenu:

- Photos, names and possibly email addresses of key people—those most likely to be making contact with visitors.
- Giving / donations: People expect to be able to give online. If you have a case for support for a fundraising campaign, it could be downloaded here. Remember, some people think churches only want their money, so avoid reinforcing this misconception.
- Prayer: Include details of regular prayer. Invite prayer requests via the contact page, if you'll act on them.
- Community action: To demonstrate your commitment to the local community, include links to local charities or support organisations. Some people will come to a church website specifically motivated by physical and emotional need. They are looking for practical help. Can you point them in the right direction? Can you give links to other websites, phone numbers, providing next steps for the broken and hurting?
- World mission. Please be extremely careful not to name people or the countries they work in if this would endanger their work. Lives are put at risk and works destroyed by churches that publicise information. To be clear, this sort of information

should never ever be on a church website, even on password-protected pages.

What's going on / Activities / Church life / Community / Events / Get involved / Get connected

This is where you showcase everything that goes on during the week. Don't forget to include a mention of Sunday services, with times. Photos, names and faces are a bonus. But ask: what's the subtext? Is it 'Look, we're so busy'? or is it 'There's a place for you to meet people—you are welcome here.'

By all means list everything you do, but the purpose is not to show off; it is to enable people to get involved if they wish. A 'call to action' with every description of a group or activity can be as simple as 'Everyone is welcome. Contact us, or just turn up.'

This page *must* be up to date, otherwise people may turn up to a closed door. You may be able to make it less time-sensitive by using general statements: 'Contact us for the next start date'; 'Check our weekly news sheet for the next venue' (with a link); 'We normally meet every Thursday in term time'.

Enable people to sign up for courses and events online, even through a contact form. If they need to pay too, Eventbrite is useful for many churches.

Many churches include a free Google calendar in this section.

Visitors / New to us? / First visit / New to church? / Our services / Mass times / What to expect

This is where you reassure people who've never been to church that you're not a bunch of weirdos, and give them the basic information they need. Reduce anxiety by explaining what happens in a typical service, what people wear, the style of music, how long people stay, exactly what the children and young people can expect to experience, some reassurance about safeguarding perhaps, and of course a mention of the excellent quality of coffee afterwards. These pages will be the most important on the whole site for some visitors.

Our history / Facilities / Weddings / Baptisms / Funerals

If your church is a place of historical interest or particularly photogenic for summer weddings, give the relevant information, but perhaps also link to other pages for the broader context of who you are. If the building is not of special interest, all this information could go in the 'About us' section, but avoid using the website as a dumping ground for irrelevant archive. That's not what it's for.

If your church is a tourist destination—or perhaps a destination on a game like Pokemon Go[34]—it is an opportunity to show that you are a welcoming space, on your website, in your building and using every means at your disposal.

Media / Talks / Teaching / Video / Downloads

Increasingly, people who don't come to church will listen to or watch talks online. They may even watch live services, through projects like the Church of England's 'ChurchLive'. Make it easy for them. Podcasts are free and easy to set up if you're already recording your talks.

Some churches enable comments, but proceed with caution: you'll need someone to moderate them carefully. A simple video showing what happens on a Sunday, or a welcome chat from a church leader, can work well, even if it's fairly simple.

Photos / Newsletter / Blog / Magazine / News sheets / Stories

If you have 'Photos' as a menu item, it will draw in the curious. Blogs can contain anything you like and can work well as digital magazines, but they need to be kept up to date. Not all church leaders are great writers, and not all of them want to write. There shouldn't be any expectation of a blog. It can become an enormous and unnecessary burden for some people. For others it's a joy. Church leaders have limited capacity and should be released to play to their strengths. Some will prefer to speak briefly to a camera rather than write a long article.

Church on the Inside in this series looks more closely at magazines, news sheets and blogs. One practical note: if you're offering downloads, make sure they are saved as PDF ('portable document format'), never in Word or Publisher, so that they can be opened by anyone on any computer system.

Most powerful of all are stories from people within the church: testimonies of faith, testimonials of how the church has helped, or quotes from people who come to groups or activities. You don't need photos or full names.

Charities do this in fundraising all the time: they tell a story. Churches neglect storytelling at their peril. As Jesus demonstrated, a story of a life transformed endures in the imagination far longer than dry information. It contributes to what marketers call 'social proof', the evidence that others have been on the same journey and had a positive experience.

Gathering information for a website can open doors to people sharing from the front at church, which can also be very powerful.

Contact

The reason people use forms and those funny little boxes to 'prove you're not a robot' (Captcha or similar) is to avoid spam emails.[35] Unprotected email addresses on websites get added to lists by spammers (and receive lots and lots of sometimes very offensive emails). This is part of the reason it's risky to put people's email addresses on a website. So opt for a form—and also include opening times, service times, address, directions, parking or public transport advice, accessibility and phone numbers. You can include a Google map for free.

People will use church website contact forms to email about everything from hall hire for parties to hellfire rants. I know. I've seen them. Sometimes there'll be a heartbreaking plea for prayer or advice. Think very carefully about who will check the email and when. They are not necessarily always the best person to respond. Be aware that con artists will send emails deliberately targeting churches. For the heartbreaking contacts or the crazy ones, email may not be the most pastorally appropriate way to continue the conversation.

Contacting through a website is not the same as speaking to an individual, and it's perfectly reasonable, even with smartphones, only to check email in office hours. You may want to state this clearly on the 'Contact' page.

Plan your content

Writing for websites is different from writing for print. You need short clear sentences, an 'active' not 'passive' voice ('Father Kevin welcomes you' rather than 'You're welcomed by Father Kevin') and no jargon. Hopefully most of your pages will not need regular changes: in web parlance, they'll be 'static'. But there is an opportunity to show what's coming up soon and, crucially, what's coming up after that.

See it as a 'rhythm of mission'. If you get most visitors at Christmas, what might interest them in the new year? Is there anything to motivate Easter visitors to connect with you at some point during the summer? The question is always 'What next?' It doesn't need to be a course, activity or service. It might be a midweek group, or even signing up to receive regular texts or emails from the church or from some of the excellent national campaigns that provide through-the-year engagement.[36]

As well as up-to-date content, you'll need software updates. Has this been discussed with your website provider? Will they know what to do if the software crashes? All processes and plans should be written down somewhere. Don't be one of those churches where the key person disappears and no one else knows what to do.

Be visible

Here are some ways not to 'hide your light under a bushel':

- Domain name (and email): as we've said, make it as close to your church name and place as possible, with email addresses to match.

- Put your website at the bottom of every email, on the noticeboard and on everything you print.
- Ask local organisations, church networks or church members to include your website as a link on their social media and on their websites. Add the church to local directories and parent forums (but ask them not to include your email address, to avoid spam). Also make sure you're on the church directories listed in Chapter 4 (Toolkit). This will help your Google rankings.
- Consider Google AdWords. It's not as scary as it sounds. You can specify that you want to spend only a certain amount—for example, £3 a day for two weeks, ideal for a special course or service. Remember the church in London who ensured that their marriage course advert appeared when people searched for 'divorce lawyer near me'? AdWords grants are also available for registered charities, with various eligibility criteria.[37]

Search Engine Optimisation (SEO) is the obsession of many web-based companies. It's all about getting on the first page of Google searches.

Your aim is not to compete with the rest of the world. Your aim is to be found easily.

Here are some simple church SEO tips:

- Include at the start of your home page your name, location, the word 'church', key people, activities or groups.
- Use phrases you think people are likely to use when searching for your church—for example, 'Baptist church East London' or 'Catholic church in Hove school catchment area'.
- Make sure your website builder is 'tagging' every page with a title that is factual, concise and unique to that page. You will be able to see this under the page description in your website builder or content management system.

Ideally every page should also have a 'meta description', a short summary of the content. If it's blank, a search engine will just use the first 160 characters it finds on the page, which may be irrelevant. You can also make the URL specific (www. churchname.org.uk/children rather than www. churchname.org.uk/X3xbr).

Instead of using 'Click here' as a link, link the whole phrase—for example, 'Find out more about Messy Church in Swindon here'.

If you want to attract people who don't go to church, make sure you use the sort of language they might use when searching for a church—for example, 'community group', 'family activities', 'relationship support', 'spiritual questions', 'why is church so important', even 'why is church so hard'.[38] Uncomfortably, if you type into Google 'why is church so…' the next word it predicts is 'boring'. Why is church so boring? Does it need to be? Should it be? Good question!

Hopefully this has given you fuel to take the next step in reaching out through a website.

There are plenty of resources to help you in the next chapter. You can also visit www.cpo.org.uk/toolkit.

4

Toolkit

All these links and more can be found at www.cpo.org.uk/toolkit. Where you see 'bit.ly', it is a shortcut link to type in.

Website providers

- www.church123.com
- www.churchedit.com
- www.churchesaliveonline.com
- www.churchinsight.com
- www.interactivechurch.org.uk
- www.samevine.co.uk
- www.ukchurches.co.uk

Many of these sites also offer advice and blogs. For example, for advice on church websites and evangelism, see www.church123.com/design.

UK church directories

- www.achurchnearyou.com (Church of England only)

- www.findachurch.co.uk (listing over 45,000 UK churches)
- www.searchchurch.co.uk (listing churches that are visitor-focused or that run courses like Alpha)

UK church communications blogs

- www.churchtrain.uk
- www.premierdigital.org.uk
- www.samevine.co.uk/blog
- www.churchesaliveonline.com/blog

Church website and administration providers like Church123, ChurchEdit, ChurchApp and ChurchBox also provide blog and training content.

US church communications blogs

- www.churchtechtoday.com
- www.churchmarketingsucks.com
- www.churchm.ag
- www.thecreativepastor.com
- www.churchjuice.com
- www.prochurchtools.com

You can sign up for updates from these blogs. If the quantity of information is overwhelming, schedule a time to review, or stick to the most relevant one.

Information about Christianity

- www.christianity.org.uk
- www.lookingforGod.com
- www.justpray.uk
- www.alpha.org
- www.rejesus.co.uk
- www.knowmystory.co.uk

Text message providers and advice

- www.clicksms.co.uk
- www.firetext.co.uk
- www.flocknote.com/blog/church-text-messaging
- www.textlocal.com

The church online administration providers listed below may also be able to help with text messaging.

Apps and email tools

- www.piota.co.uk (for church and school apps)
- www.mailchimp.com (for graphic emails, with free options)
- www.dotmailer.com

Survey tools

- www.doodle.com
- www.formstack.com

- www.smartsurvey.co.uk
- www.surveymonkey.net
- www.getfeedback.com
- Google Forms (part of Google Drive)

Church online administration providers

- www.churchbox.co.uk
- www.churchapp.co.uk
- www.churchinsight.com
- www.iknowchurch.co.uk

For free well-known collaborative tools with plenty of online support, try Google Docs and Dropbox.

Church online giving/fundraising

- www.give.net is part of Stewardship, a Christian charity who will give you advice on all areas of church finance.
- Public fundraising tools like www.justgiving.com, www.virginmoneygiving.com, www.gofundme. com and www.easyfundraising.org.uk can work for churches, or try bit.ly/2duKIlg for advice.
- JustTextGiving enables giving via text and is free for charities.

- Pingit is a way of transferring money via mobile phones. Expect huge growth in mobile payments.
- www.leptongiving.com is an app to help churches with giving, even enabling contactless payments.
- The resources and advice at www.parishresources.org.uk are meant for Church of England churches but could be applied to all churches.
- *The UK Church Fundraising Handbook* by Maggie Durran (Canterbury Press, 2003) remains an excellent printed resource for churches running fundraising campaigns.
- For text giving, try Push Pay and get.tithe.ly.

Free images for websites

- Freely: www.freelyphotos.com
- Unsplash: www.unsplash.com
- Wiki Commons: commons.wikimedia.org
- Flickr 'Creative Commons': flickr.com/creativecommons
- Google: in Google Images, click 'Search tools', then 'Usage rights', and choose from those 'labelled for reuse'
- www.photopin.com
- Stock Up: www.sitebuilderreport.com/stock-up
- churchm.ag/unsplash-alternatives
- www.morguefile.com

Advice on church copyright and data protection

London Diocese's parish communications toolkit has up-to-date sections on copyright and on data: bitly.com/ParishCommsToolkit.

On data protection, churches are subject to the rules set out by www.ico.gov.uk. A helpful briefing for churches is at bitly.com/StewardshipData.

For advice on music, lyrics and video, contact CCLI (01323 436100; ccli.com).

Tools for creating website graphics

- pablo.buffer.com
- spark.adobe.com (also useful for videos)
- canva.com

Links to good church websites

- www.premierdigital.org.uk/awards
- www.3sixtycreative.com/10-of-the-best-church-websites
- www.vandelaydesign.com/best-church-websites
- https://prochurchtools.com/best-church-websites

Examples of online outreach

- www.40acts.org.uk
- yesheis.com
- Bible apps like YouVersion

To build a picture of the UK church

- www.greatcommission.co.uk from the Evangelical Alliance
- Talking Jesus: www.talkingjesus.org
- Bob Jackson, *What Makes Churches Grow?* (Church House Publishing, 2015)

To build a picture of your locality

- The Centre for Theology & Community has a list of sources of local information for churches, such as those mapping poverty or religious affiliation, with questions for churches to use in reflecting on this data. Visit www.theology-centre.org/my-context.
- You can find a summary report for your neighbourhood from the Office for National Statistics (www.neighbourhood.statistics.gov.uk/dissemination), or see the same information brilliantly colour-coded and searchable at Datashine (www.datashine.org.uk).

- A free trial of Acorn (www.acorn.caci.co.uk) will describe your neighbours down to where they're likely to shop, what they're likely to buy and how they use their smartphone.
- If you're in a rural area, the Arthur Rank Centre has a course for profiling local needs and creating priorities for action: bit.ly/1hHFiBr.
- If you're brave enough to use a questionnaire to find out what people think of your church, sample questions might include:

  - *How long have you lived in the area?*
  - *What local services do you use?*
  - *What do you think are some of the issues locally?*
  - *Have you ever visited or connected with [name of church] in any way?*
  - *Did you know that the church offers [list activities]?*
  - *Would you find it useful to be notified of future courses/events?*
  - *Would you like prayer?*

Recommended further reading

- www.rapiddevelopment.org.uk/resources
- www.dur.ac.uk/codec
- www.premierdigital.org.uk
- www.churchtrain.uk/resources

Notes

1 *Talking Jesus: Perceptions of Jesus, Christians and evangelism in England* (Evangelical Alliance, HOPE, Church of England, 2015).

2 Prof Linda Woodhead undertook the survey of religion for Lancaster University with YouGov in 2016. Full results can be found by searching for 'Lancaster religion' at www.yougov.com. There is also a summary at www.lancaster.ac.uk/news/articles/2016/why-no-religion-is-the-new-religion.

3 Ofcom, *Adults' Media Use and Attitudes: Report 2015*: bit.ly/1E3fFyO.

4 General Synod, *Report from the Archbishops' Evangelism Task Group* (The Archbishops' Council, 2016), p. 3: bit.ly/2ddwjrs.

5 bit.ly/2dD2OhR.

6 www.mumsnet.com/Talk/am_i_being_unreasonable/a1499475-to-be-amazed-at-people-going-to-church.

7 Prof Linda Woodhead, 'Lancaster religion', www.yougov.com.

8 Steve Aisthorpe, 'Investigating the Invisible Church': www.resourcingmission.org.uk/sites/default/files/downloads/Investigating%20the%20invisible%20church.pdf.

9 Steve Aisthorpe, *The Invisible Church* (St Andrew Press, 2016).

10 Examples are www.life.church and www.
    londoninternetchurch.org.uk, aiming for a global
    reach and even a global community.

11 Richard Reising, *Church Marketing 101* (Baker, 2006),
    p. 41.

12 Brady Shearer, '4 Church Website Stats You Can't
    Afford to Ignore': www.prochurchtools.com/4-
    church-website-stats-you-cant-afford-to-ignore.

13 Office of National Statistics, *Internet Users in the UK:
    2016*: www.ons.gov.uk/businessindustryandtrade/
    itandinternetindustry/bulletins/internetusers/2016.

14 Sara Batts, *Informing, inviting or ignoring?
    Understanding how English Christian churches use
    the internet* (University of Loughborough, 2013),
    p. 237. You can read the full version at
    bit.ly/2cNIqhO and Sara's blog on the process at
    https://phdinprogress.wordpress.com.

15 For example, try Joy Jittaun Moore, 'Social Media
    and the Church: Communication among the
    masses', with a reading list: bit.ly/2dVtyOX.

16 Correct as of 2016.

17 Pope Benedict XVI, *Social Networks: Portals of truth
    and faith; new spaces for evangelization* (Libreria
    Editrice Vaticana, 2013).

18 www.fromevidencetoaction.org.uk.

19 For a more comprehensive free audit tool, try the
    old but useful list at www.internetevangelismday.
    com/church-site-design.php.